To

....

From

PETER

THE CRUISE SHIP

and the Pirates

To Callie

Captain Hans

Written by
Captain Hans Mateboer

Illustrated by
Michael LaDuca

It is warm and sunny in the Caribbean Sea. Peter happily sails along. He blows his horn, and sings a song.

TOOT!

TOOT!

He meets Rusty, his old friend. "Howdie, Rusty!"

"Hello Peter! Good to see you!" Rusty shouts back across the water.

In the distance Peter spots the "Hazy Islands". They look eerie and he stops whistling. He wants to sail by very quietly.

"Ooohhh, it's like someone is watching me."

He picks up speed as fast as he can, like a mouse scurrying from a cat.

5

"Help! Help me please! They are trying to get me!…"

What a relief to have passed that frightening place.

But wait! What's that? He hears someone calling in the distance behind him.

He turns around to see who that could be.

GET HIM TOO!

A beautiful sailing ship races by, closely trailed by.......pirates!!

"Who are you?" he shouts. "I'm Creola! Watch out for them!"

The pirates have seen Peter and now they take off after him.

"Whoa! That's four against one. I'd better get out of here!"

"Run, Creola, run!" Peter shouts. "Hide behind the small islands over there."

Boom...boom!! The pirates are trying real hard to get him.

Fluke the Whale has heard the racket above him.

"Can I help you, Peter!?"

"You'd better hide, Fluke. You can't do anything against pirates!"

Peter and Creola are hiding.
"Sssshhh, be quiet," he whispers as
he peeks around the corner.

12

Bandit is angry. He can't find Peter and Creola. He yells at the other pirates.

"You, Salty Dog, check behind that island, and you, Sloppy, why are you always so slow!"

When all the pirates are looking in another direction, Peter and Creola make a run for it.

But Bandit discovers their attempt to escape.

14

"There they go! Haa! Now we will get those two."

All four pirates turn around to chase them.

creola

Cuba

Creola is getting tired and lags behind. Peter throws a rope to pull her along.

"We need help!" he pants. "Toot!! Toot! Help! TooooooT!!...."

BANDIT

creola

PETER

SLOPPY

iola

Puerto RIco

St. Thomas

St. Maarten

Antigua

Guadaloupe

Dominica

Martinique

St. Lucia

Barbados

TOOT!

TOOT!

TOOT!

TOOT!

TOOT!

PUSH

GULP

He toots his horn as loud
as he can and is heard
throughout the
Caribbean Sea.

SLICK

Grenada

17

Trinidad

TOOT!

TOOT!

TOOT!

In the harbor, Push is helping Gulp.
They hear a cry for help.

"Quick, Push, you go ahead. I'll follow.
I'm slow with this heavy cargo of oil,"
Gulp says.

Slick the container ship hears Peter's toots also.

"It's Peter! He's in distress. I better see if I can help him!"

TOOT!

TOOT!

TOOT!

HELP!

"Faster guys!" Push shouts, anxious to locate Peter.

He knows that Peter would not ask for help if it weren't very urgent.

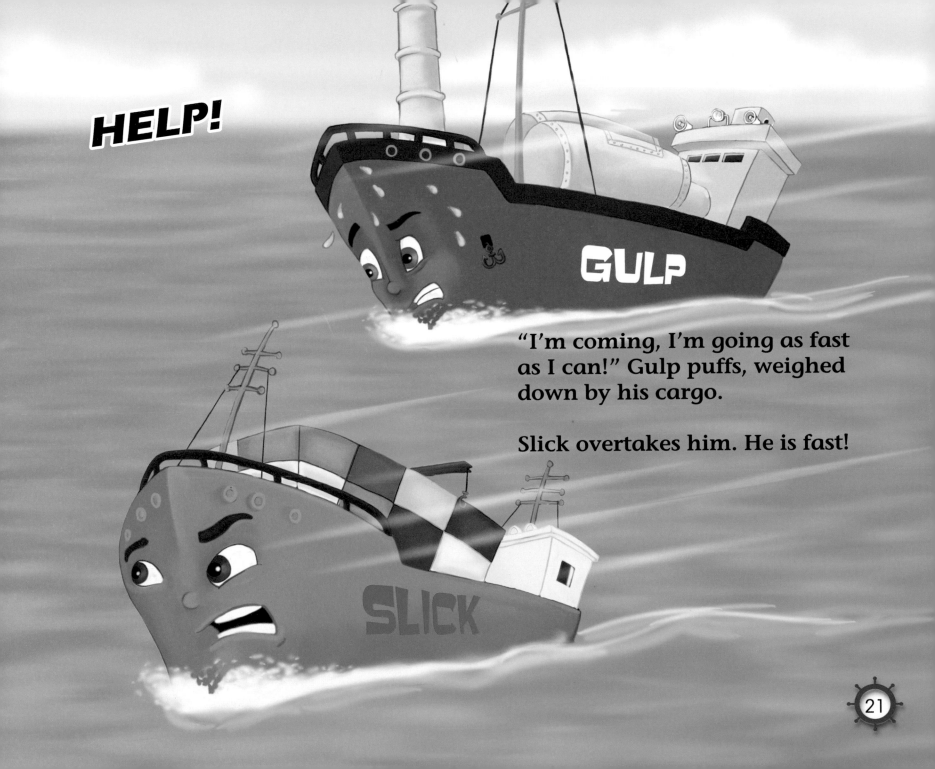

HELP!

"I'm coming, I'm going as fast as I can!" Gulp puffs, weighed down by his cargo.

Slick overtakes him. He is fast!

Push runs straight by Peter and smashes into Bandit at full speed.

"Ouch..that hurts!" Bandit cries. "Look what you did, you broke my mast!"

THUMP

OUCH!!!

CRASH

"It's your own fault!" Push grumbles.

22

Slick and Gulp are not far behind. Creola is very happy and cheers them.

The pirates, like all bullies, are just cowards. They panic when they see Peter's friends.

Salty Dog wants to run away so fast that he bangs into Booty. "Aauuww, get out of my way!" he screams.

CLUNK!!!

RUN GUYS!

Sloppy is so confused that he starts running in circles. Bandit smashes into him.

Peter and his friends laugh so hard that they have tears in their eyes.

Peter and Creola are relieved.

Creola blinks her eyes and stops laughing. "Thank you guys, that was a close call. Especially you, Push. You are all scratched and your eye is swelling."

Push blushes at Creola's praise. "Aaww...I don't mind. Tugboats get scratches often."

Together they decide to take some time off and rest in the harbor of a tropical island.

"Wow, I think you all did a great job! I'm sure those pirates learned their lesson," Peter tells them.

"We'll have a good time here. It's such a nice place." Creola sighs. "I could stay forever."

Too soon it's time to go. Gulp has to deliver his cargo of oil, and Slick is very busy too.

"Goodbye Creola," Peter shouts. "Goodbye Push, Goodbye Gulp and Slick! See you all soon!!"

"Phew!! that was quite an adventure. I never ran so fast in my life. I wonder what's next? Being at sea is always exciting."

ISBN 978-0-9759487-4-3
Published by Captain's Publishing
www.captainspublishing.com
Printed in the United States of America
CPSIA Compliance Information: Batch # 0909.
For further information contact
RJ Communications, NY NY, 800-621-2556